Advance Praise for:

FRAGMENTS OF LIGHT

"It's true that KB Ballentine is an admirably precise descriptive poet, loyal to the conditions of the natural world: "Leaves crunch underfoot/as I trek to the lake. Brief barks/from the other side, then silence." But it's a limited truth. Her *imagination*—inhering in verbs and nouns where it does its best work—invites nature "indoors," into her subjective life: "The falcon's body arced by whorls /of wind"; "summers were best, daylight yawned early, /stayed awake late"; and (among my favorites) "in the woods my boots bruise Johnny / jump-ups and forget-me-nots." In the first case, "whorls" renders the invisible visible; in the second, personification animates, with friendly wit, a child's delight in the lengthening days of summer; the third marshals even more subtle techniques: diction both literal and figurative, a provocative enjambment, and the power of the *accurately named*. Indeed, it's the *names* of those flowers that suggest their resistance, or protest, against the bruising boots.

So, enjoy being "seduced by the light" of Ballentine's keen observations, but also read these poems alert to their osmosis of the world into the self: "Breathe in, breathe out. Breathe," she instructs. With understated grace, that's what KB Ballentine's poems do."

--Steven Cramer
Goodbye to the Orchard
MFA Creative Writing Program Director, Lesley University

"KB Ballentine sheds new light on old light. Her words of wisdom make your spirit come alive and travel the back roads of her mind where you encounter the seasons of her genius."

--Margaret Britton Vaughn
Poet Laureate of Tennessee

"KB Ballentine's poems display a painter's sense of the ever-shifting, never-the-same light as it reveals, caresses, sometimes stuns. Light depicts both the outer natural world as well as the inner life of observer/speaker of these poems and exposes painful experiences as in the lines: "I've buried a sister, a friend./ When was the family string cut—/who brought the knife?" And not to be missed are the seasons of the moon, surely some of the best poems in *Fragments of Light*."

--Jeff Daniel Marion, *Father*

FRAGMENTS OF LIGHT

Books by KB Ballentine

Gathering Stones

FRAGMENTS OF LIGHT

KB BALLENTINE

KNOXVILLE, TENNESSEE

Celtic Cat Publishing
2654 Wild Fern Lane
Knoxville, Tennessee 37931
www.celticcatpublishing.com

Manufactured in the United States of America
Design by Greyhound Books
Cover photograph by KB Ballentine

We look forward to hearing from you. Please send comments about this book to the publisher at the address above. For information about special educational discounts and discounts for bulk purchases, please contact Celtic Cat Publishing.

ISBN: 978-0-9819238-1-9

Library of Congress Control Number: 2009928127

Publication Acknowledgements

"Brushstroke"
2008 Poets' Guide to New Hampshire (printed under the title "Otter Pond")

"Countdown"
Dorothy Sargent Rosenberg Prize Winner 2007

"Dante Meets Katrina, 2005"
2006 Joy Harjo Award Finalist

"Daybreak at the Old City Park"
MO: Writings from the River Spring 2009

"Elemental"
Bent Pin Spring 2007

"Frost Line"
Bent Pin Spring 2009 (printed under the title "The Dawning")

"Hunter's Moon"
Bent Pin Spring 2009

"Pink Moon"
River Poets Journal Spring 2009

"September Woods"
Naugatuck River Review Summer 2009

"St Augustine, Early Morning"
Sea Stories January 2008

"Summer in Climax"
MO: Writings from the River Spring 2007 (printed under the title "Climax")

PERSONAL ACKNOWLEDGEMENTS

Many thanks to the people who have helped me make this second collection what it is. To my workshop partners Helga Kidder, Penny Dyer, John Mannone, and Finn Bille for insightful suggestions and for providing other sets of eyes; to the various workshop groups who provided ideas and revision techniques: Chattanooga Writers' Guild, Knoxville Writers' Guild, and Tennessee Mountain Writers', Inc.; to the dedicated monthly Open Mic members who listened to several revisions of the same poems and kept encouraging me; for the love and support of the Lesley ladies, Kenny Allred, Kristi Walker, Valerie Cannon, David Austin, Stephanie Blank, my RCHS and BN co-workers and my students; to Steven Cramer and Jim Johnston for believing in my work and pushing me to do my best; to friends who have consistently prayed for me, and to the people who have passed through my life providing inspiration and story for my work. And to my family for always being by my side. I could not have pulled this off without all of you.

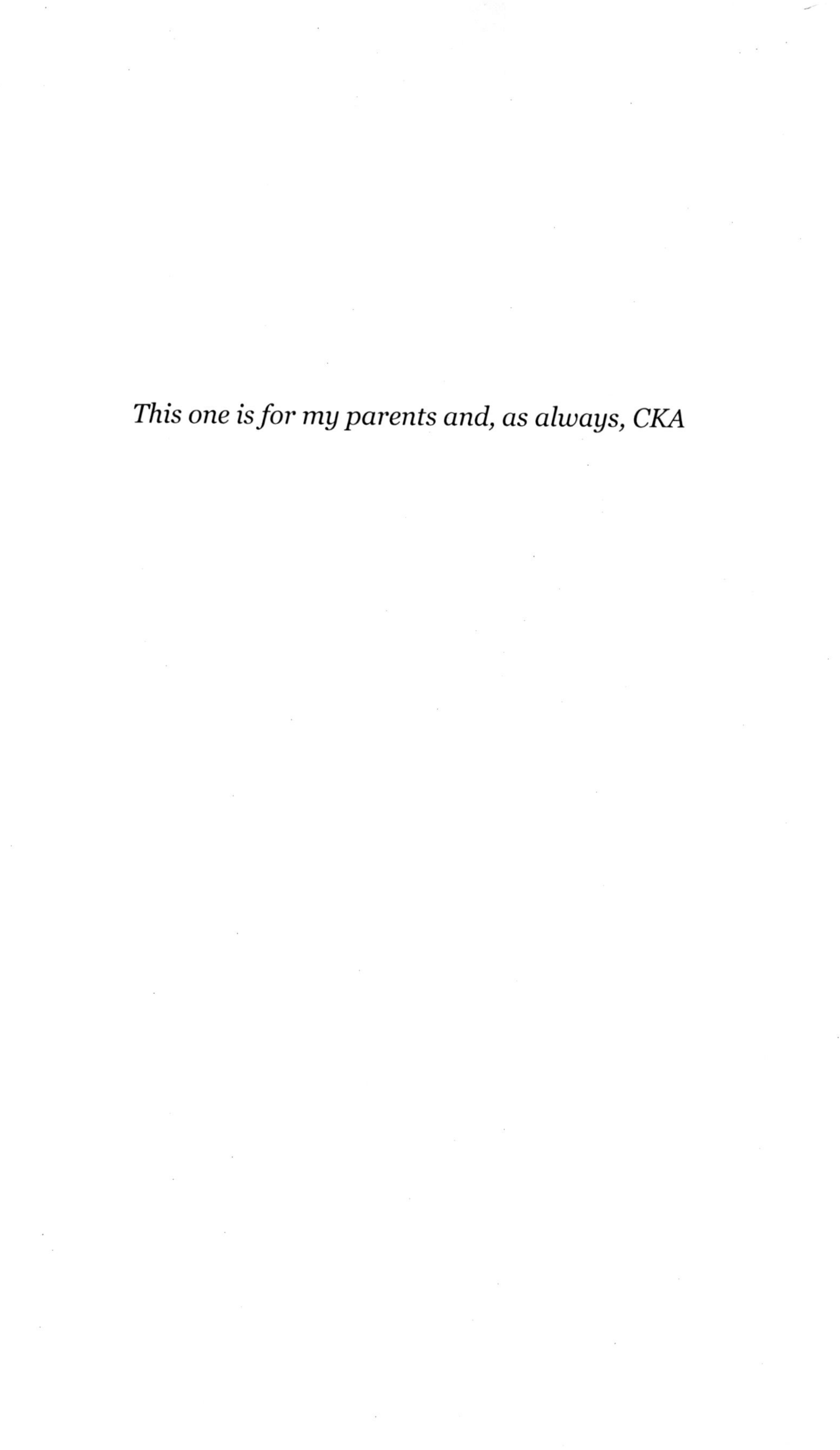

This one is for my parents and, as always, CKA

Author's Foreword

> "To man, that was in th' evening made,
> Stars gave the first delight;
> Admiring, in the gloomy shade,
> Those little drops of light."

> --*An Apology for Having Loved Before*
> Edmund Waller

Light stalking shadow. Spring chasing winter. *Fragments of Light* explores cycles, how light and shadow affect nature and people. Begin the journey and chase the changing months in the moon poems. Linger within them as language wraps around allusion. Discover the various names for each full moon.

Follow as each morning dawns with hope and promise; reflect as night descends and "shadows stretch/ hoary fingers" ("Cold Moon"). Pursue the ambiguous, intangible feelings that are as difficult to grasp as shifting light.

Move with me through the season's shadow and light. Each requires the other. Adversity attempts to cover light with its darkness. But, though the moon waxes and wanes, fragments of light are never extinguished. Continue to reach for that light throughout the weeks and months ahead – homing towards journey's end.

↗ Winter Solstice

♓ Vernal Equinox

Ⅱ Summer Solstice

♍ Autumnal Equinox

WINTER SOLSTICE

STARGAZING

A girl could get dizzy looking
at the stars, fireballs of flickering
gases consuming their own energy.
Disharmony, chaos, a pulse out
of tempo – closer, farther away
in the silence. One fixed point
would do.

       The choice is where to look.
Sky spangles with light, closer
in the cold, clear air. Hemmed in,
dazzled by darkness flaming in cold
pinpricks of fire. Breathe in, breathe out.
Breathe.

Starshine

Mountain air chills
this time of year
We spent the day chasing
the sun till it sank
leaving us alone

Big Dipper, globed moon
our only guides
We anchor ourselves
onto hard cold rock
glad the river isn't higher
faster

A bat zigzags the sky
wings throb a faster cadence
than bouldered riverbed
Turning three bodies into one
is a trick as magical
as striking stones to create fire

Time blinks by with each
ascending star
too many   to count
too few   to light
the way

So we wait
while the moon mounts
and we measure
the stars with new
vision

WOLF MOON
January

The moon howls its rings
as it tracks the trees, stalks
bare branches of red
maples, chasing scarecrow
shadows across the yard.

Leaves crunch underfoot
as I trek to the lake. Brief barks
from the other side, then silence.

The overturned skiff trembles
like an exposed rabbit
on the shore, gray timber nuzzling
sand, water snapping wood.
Light scatters darkness,

keen for the hunt.

UMBRELLAS

Black blooms bob ahead,
night falling on this gray
lidded day. Street lights,
head lights can't decipher
shadowy figures under
their moving shelters, bodies
wrapped, scarved against
this winter twilight.

You offer me cover,
protection from icy tears
that staccato the awnings,
the road. I accept, and we
are shuttered together –
a *tête-à-tête*. Horns, sirens,
rain recede to whispers.
Our shoulders scuff,
breaths feathering the dark.

Snow Moon
February

Gnawing at midnight's black rind,
the moon glazes crusts of snow.
Fat flakes beard branches, grow
coats, fleece as powder freezes
in drifts and mounds, threatening
mini-avalanches. Vapor rises
from the lake, burns the blackness
white. The rest of night holding
its breath.

ANSWERS

How alone my grandfather must be
in a grave for two occupied by one.
Through the gray smooth stone
I ask him, *What of loneliness?*

He says loneliness isn't saw grass
sifting wind or mirrored blue of sea
and sky. It isn't standing still
on a crowded sidewalk or playing

solitaire. He says it is the arm chair,
empty when your wife leaves early
for work, your son's sterile room
when college calls.

It is the only child
saying goodbye to her last parent.

COUNTDOWN

A spear of light scratches
the dark clouds overhead and time stands
still – movement arrested
by a well of pain.
Sutures of a life re-stitched
over broken
memories have burst open
like a robin's egg smashing to ground.
Carnations bought for your bedside
will now decorate your new home –
dark and earthy.

Time
once again
ticks toward oblivion,
but I concentrate
on the carrots I will cook tonight:

they were your favorite.

THE WILL

When I'm dead, don't put me in a box –
never one for narrow spaces,
even satin lining can't make
those borders more comfortable.

No, when I'm dead, burn my body –
      alter me to ash. Then, in a jar,
      carry me to the mountains
      whose ridges brood like me.
Or to the ocean where I was born.

There's nothing to send with me,
      except maybe your songs, baritoned
      and echoing in the shower
or your music, guitar-calloused fingers
      thrumming my body in melodic rhythm.

And when you let me go – remember,
you must let me go – let it be
as the sun rises, gentling
around you with warm embrace.

WORM MOON
March

Daylight burrows as night crawls
across the sky, the moon a crust
of bread. Thawing fields stiffen
in snow, congeal without warm
streams wriggling from the sun.

Fox tracks scratch the white –
a crow's wing like a shadow
under the stars. Layered in dirt,
the earthworm begins to budge.
In the quiet a robin trembles,
tree sap rises.

Morning After

Hills ripple the distance.
A crow jabs blued
skies with sable wings,
his caw stunning the dawn.
He spies gold in furrowed
earth, a shriveled kernel
left in Brody's field.

From the porch I watch
you leave, dissolve in mist.
Frost crumples buds straining
to taste air, light futile
these early winter days.

Holding On, Letting Go

Sunrise blushes the sky,
peach yellowing into blue
as the tide rolls in. Salt
spatters my legs, scratches
where it sticks. Condos,
hotels come into view,
and I backtrack, trudging
toward the pier. A couple
holding hands, a jogger
with her dog my only
companions.

You came in late last night.
I heard you shower, felt
you slide into bed, body
damp and clean like this early
air that stabs my nostrils,
prickles my throat. The dog
runs into the shallows, barks
at waves, snaps at what
he can't see.

IN THE WAITING

Silence ricochets
through these white woods,
dewy flakes tumbling
from vanilla skies
that eclipse sunlight
laboring to paint
this colorless world
into brilliance.

Oblivion wins:
clouds gather
beyond the trees,
moisture thickens the air.
An exuberant cardinal,
plumage bright
in the snow, chatters
into nothingness.

Dubious at my appearance
he darts off among the gray
sentinels standing
over this cemetery of silence.

THRESHOLD

A white inferno, the moon annuls night,
delays as dawn paints horizon pink
and orange. Frost traces edge of sand,
skims tide – seaweed strangles
the beach. I step farther along the strand,
burrow into your Rutgers sweatshirt
and watch yawning day awake.

Sea oats tangle, nod. Surf slugs shore,
vacuums with each wave's wintering suck
and spew. Spray flies in salty blasts, snaps
on rocks down shore. I turn my back on the sea,
the sun – hair and wind stinging my eyes .

Broken Question

Clouds growl and bellow
shadows rob ice-black night
of blood and fire
Decaying moans sweep
like bitter wind shaking
through the universe

A powerful storm
piercing as death rips
my soul and I am left
with your ghost

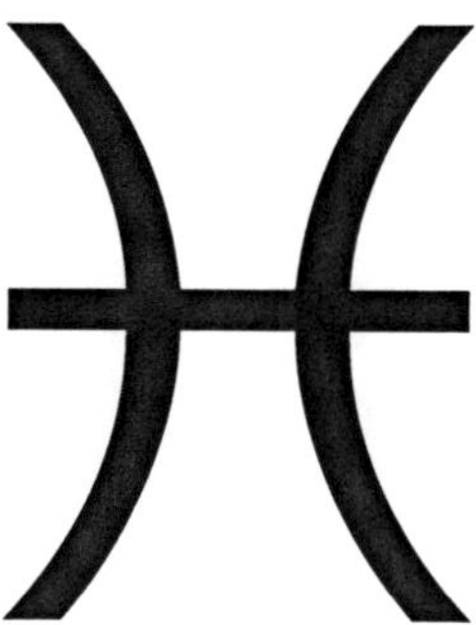

VERNAL EQUINOX

PINK MOON
April

The sunburned sky slides
behind the mountain, shadows
stretch toward night. Violets
and bleeding hearts' dark
petals sweeten grass. Crocus
and snowdrop flicker like pearls,
phlox crawls from wood to lawn.
Clouds crack the moon, an egg
suspended in a bowl of stars.

BRUSHSTROKE

Silent as light
geese approach the pond and settle
a shadow on its surface, ripples
reverberating into nothing.
The schism of night and day
has begun, moon paling in the pink
dawn fading star by star.

I crave this vision of Watteau
when the world pummels with need
and slander. Or maybe Carravaggio's
chiaroscuro on canvas – allowing a glimpse
of the important, and what is not.

THE GOBLIN BEE

– after Dickinson's "If You Were
Coming in the Fall"

Streets sleep. The television glares the couch blue,
but not the corners where shadows lurk like flies.
Fall and winter seemed static worlds of blue and gray.

New spring buds sprinkle the greening lawn
like crayons tossed from a drawer.
                                        I missed your call,

the ringing disguised by sparrows squeaking
and flittering, afraid of crows. Forget-me-nots
blued the sky, trembled as I scooped dirt for tulips.

I've dropped a stitch of chains since you left, circle
widening, ball unraveling. How can I cup time,
toss it like rinds till you come back to me?

Pushing into darkness, cold light – blue halo, wings –
flickers in the night. From the screen, a faint buzz.

DUSK

Swallows settle, feathers quivering into silence.
Somewhere past the fading light a dog yaps,
receives an answer. Dogwood blossoms
punctuate twilight, white dotting the line of oak
and pine like strings of pearls.

Inside, gray curtains
wave in the same April draft, and questions stretch
into the stillness of the house. Book open, unread,
I stare out at the hinge of day.

Announcing Spring

Little League Cardinals scurry
outfield, and a Norfolk Southern
engine screeches, rattles the dew
damp seats, a transient earthquake
shaking husks that litter the bleachers.

Triple Crown box car wheels squeal
like a thousand nails pitched
onto concrete, clatter the track, eclipse
the bat's whack, our cheers.

We bask in the mounting sun, glasses
glinting like mirrors. Hot dogs, pizza,
peanuts ripple the stands. Graffiti blurs
by, speeding us toward an uncertain
destination. The batter waits.

CLOCKWORK

The world outside beckons,
whispers seductive words.
Sunrays break through fog
to reveal a sky so bright a blue
my head swims with light.
Blinded, my compass swirls,
returns to the prison of walls
and rules.
       Around me,
others share the vacant stare
of the breathing dead. Thought
and life suspend, wait for ticking
hands to circle toward freedom.

WATCHING THE BREAKERS
– after Winslow Homer

Salt spray spatters
my face, and I scramble
farther up the rocks,
away from the changing tide.
Gray clouds tumble into the churning
water – black then tossing white.
Margaret holds to the water,
follows it back and forth
back and forth –
a little closer each time,
skirt hem damp
bare legs crusted with salt
yellow hair escapes
from tugging scarf.

I holler over wind and surf
but she doesn't hear. Once,
she glanced up and I motioned
her in. She turned from me
from the shore,
opened her arms –
embraced the sea.

Gold Dust

on the windshield. Brief
life flickered more
briefly. Yellow and black
flashed after a smaller,
bluer sister passing,
plunging across traffic.
Tag, you're it.

AWAKENINGS

Kaleidoscopic jolts ended. Silence
chased shuddering brakes, racketing
engine. Steam and smoke bound me,
the ditch gripping my ruined behemoth.

Car door overhead, I pushed the seatbelt
latch, falling like oil from a bottle. Waiting
school children raised me from metal fractures
then left me alone, morning bus claiming them.

My adolescent angels surrendered to its groan
and hiss, merged with faces gaping over open
windows. I limped along the asphalt, each stone,
each dandelion for once distinct. Trees tugged the sun

as finches flickered overhead, and I tried
to remember the last time I listened to their tune.
Swollen buds hung like dew and lawns plumped
green, faded cuttings tunneling the grass.

When had winter shuffled away? I thumped
the door of the nearest house, waking its widow
from forgotten loneliness and memory's kisses,
heard her creaking through the hall, watched

the door open on her withered face.

TERMINUS

28

My eyes range the heaving sea,
salt spray like shards on skin. Foam
churns, slumps the base of rocky
coast. Honey-headed gannets shriek,
black-tipped wings cede to swelling wind.

The motor drones underfoot, its
noise deadened by breaking surf.
Starboard, the other boat dips beneath
watery horizon, rolling up again for air.

Brine roils, unfurls. Air heavy, wet,
kittiwakes and puffins vanish as we head
home. For a moment, gray clouds separate,
and we are seduced by light.

Ghazal for Spring

The pond ruffles, winks in April's ice blue.
Buntings riveted in trees, jays rail blue.

Blush bouquet discarded, golden circle
severed, empty sanctuary – veil blue.

Flakes sputter through spring sky oblivious
to dogwood, redbud blossoms, lips frail blue.

Faint melody vibrates air, warblers
silent, still – riffs on piano scale blue.

Gliding thick, flurries obscure the mountain.
Daffodils stoop, magnolias hail blue.

Carry on till tomorrow, hope will win.
Wrap today's sorrow in a ball, wail blue.

DISCORD

The dog whines as thunder growls
in the waning light. Gray clouds
cement the horizon, truncate afternoon.

A breeze flicks my cheek, creases
the long grass, spits dandelion fluff.
Irises wink at garden's edge, purpling

into shadow. Rain skeins the sky.

FLOWER MOON
May

Woods edge the field, shelter
columbine and prairie clover.
A chapel spire thrusts through
pine, mountain laurel. Furrows
of open earth pucker, hungry
mouths ready to suckle grain
slumbering under stars.

The neighbor's pasture lies
fallow, births poppy and butter-
cups while wisteria mounts
forget-me-nots fading under
a milky moon.

Experiment

Wandering the beach at dawn,
the *shhh* of waves stroking shore,
I abandon all thoughts of you.
Breathe in the salt.

Kingfisher wings and wind
splinter the rosy hush. Shells
and driftwood clutter damp sand.
Seaweed shoulders the collapsing
tide, shudders in the surge.

Whiting, alewife scatter as I join
the foamy current. Cool water caresses
my body, titrating the acid lingering
in my veins.

Ache ebbing, the pulsing tide rescues
me, grasps my heart and restores it –
not whole, but fragments
                              now beating.

STRAWBERRY MOON
June

Stars, bursting like seeds from ripened
fruit, scatter the sky, rival carnival
lights as they sputter out ride by ride.
Mock orange and rose fuse with cotton
candy, lace evening shadows.

                    Strawberries
plump the verge where deer rummage
the sticky sweet. Sowing pearls,
Castor and Pollux inch off the horizon,
Cancer's blushing clusters open.

AFTERLIFE

Stars gild a margin of sky,
knots of light masquerading
as diamonds, dreams . . .

The Styx unfurls, sibilant tide
rising along banks, moored
branches swirling downstream.

The ferryman waits, head hidden,
face shrouded, wordless. To cross
is to stay – to relinquish the light.

To linger on the edge offers
a view of the heavens, just
out of reach – one hope away.

Desire

Beauty. The lake lies still before me.
Silence. I drift on currents of air.

I want to glide on ripples of water,
swim beneath the liquid sun.

You matter to me. You hold my heart
behind the mountain of the lake.

A wren *tik-tiks* and gray squirrels run
as I seek out the spirit of my soul.

Now before me you laze like the lake.
Embrace me like air, and I am yours.

THE WEEKEND

Thin rain spirals shore.
Rocks, thick-fisted, jut
the ocean. Waves sizzle,
flick and sting their froth.
Across the draining sky

gulls grunt. Crabs scuttle
through seaweed on cement
colored sand. Bloated
jellyfish shrivel, congeal
on scattered shells – hidden
thorns in this grainy garden.

Clouds dissolve. Liquid
light coalesces, strokes
a turtle as it crosses scrub.
Marigolds and sea oats
curve in drying gusts.

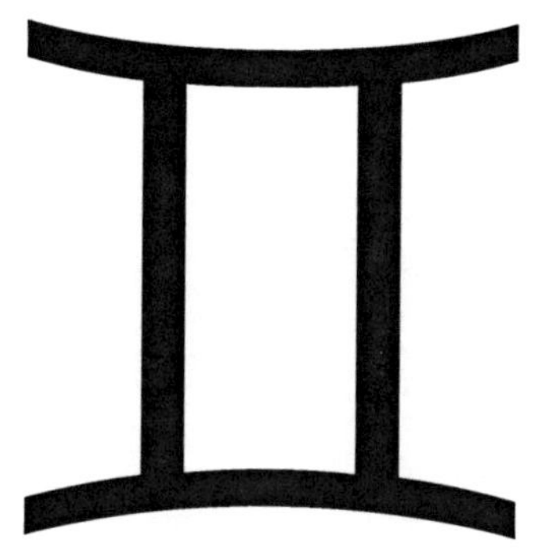

SUMMER SOLSTICE

Shat al Arab
The Fertile Crescent

She watches a blade of sun impale
the leaves, dust motes chafe the air.
No finches or orioles scatter
their notes to her ears. Even the frogs
and chimpanzees are silent.

Bamboo sways and shifts. Soil
hums, ferns sliding apart. She turns
her head, sees glossy scales unknot,
light trembling a kaleidoscope.
He rises from the mossy earth.

Teak and fig canopy thick air.
Gold bulbine shocks shadows
of purpling orchids, violets.
The woman blinks
away languid heat, asks why
he's come.

To give you the world.

Banyans creak, a cougar flashes
through the green. Somewhere
in the garden an apple falls.

AFTERWARD

The falcon's body arced by whorls
of wind, I follow his flight to the barn –
my way choked with crested wheatgrass

curving under the summer sun. Further
down, cool trees beckon, creek slicing
a crescent in the bank where poppies

and chicory tremble in the shade.
Solitary hours mingle, friends
and neighbors gone this third day

since your funeral. Wind rushes
the grass, sputters blades to whispered
applause. The falcon shrieks into blue.

In the woods my boots bruise Johnny
jump-ups and forget-me-nots.

FORGET-ME-NOT

Wind and sun squirm through treetops,
highlighting the forest floor
in a wanton, whispering mosaic. Bees hum
lazy loops, and robins pipe warnings
when I wander by. Buds rupture
into forget-me-nots, columbine blushing
brown and green. No questions here.

Fallen oaks bleed their centuries into earth
as raw heartwood shrinks, becomes brittle
like flaking scabs, crumbles into mute decay.
Beetles and worms thrive then abandon husks,
mushrooms fruiting the fertile wrecks.

DESIGN

Light frays the louvered blinds,
dust motes pepper the rays, my breath.
Crooked shadows slant the floor,
voices murmur upstairs, a succor
in the silence.

                In the garden
roses nod by hollyhocks. Air creased
by vibrating wings, risking each golden
center, hummingbirds stitch nectar cosmos
by cosmos.

RELOCATION

It's 90 degrees where you are. You shed
winter coats and sweaters when you left
this town, cold seeping into your bones
in the bare family room, muted tv glowing
blue in gathering dark.

Palm Beach wraps like a blanket around you,
warming your chilled heart. The children play,
lumber like bumble bees in swim wings
outside the pool, sipping from the nectar
of your love. You offer freely, drawing
from reserves, new-found.

Our high school photos still hug my walls,
yours burning with the house the night
your dad forgot to come home, another night
spent in mine. After twenty years you look
the same. Hair like mine in grayer shades,
skin and soul burning with the sun,
your children growing tall in the salty tide.

Buck Moon
July

Offstage, the moon peeks
from the wings – clouds
a falling curtain to thunder's
applause. Lightning spots
the night, exposing scratched
oaks – old witnesses to bucks'
rubbing, furred nubs now
beginning to bud. Hay ricks
capture right and center
in the field, and, backstage,
leaves chatter with the rain.

LIKE LIGHTNING

It wasn't fireworks, exactly –
but it might as well have been.
Intermittent flares through the tree line
brightened the expanding night.
Yellow, white. Fireflies –
who knew there could be so many?

Silent, we huddled in the car. Outside,
the air swarmed with music –
an owl shrieking across the field,
frogs' *hrrump* rising and falling
to a descant of pulsating crickets.
You pointed out the Big and Little Dippers,
traced the cups that filled each other.
Eyes searched further for Cassiopeia.
You couldn't find her.

MARGINS

Hemmed by oak and pine,
my horizon frames a portion
of the sky, bright blue. Higher,
crows circle.

One, two . . . thirteen
pairs of wings spiral through maple
leaves, shape of webbed feet.
Rain lacquers each green patch,

skates as branches lift, breeze
rousing the trees. Chattering.
Crooked shadows splay the yard.
Drops mist my face, the sun shrugs

behind a cloud. Blue unfurls
to gray, crows disappear. Peonies
sway, droop blushing faces. Inside,
I search for another margin of light.

A Summer Night

– after Winslow Homer

Sand shifted beneath our feet,
waves curled over our hems,
flashed like pearls under the moon.
The other girls laughed as we waltzed
into the tide. The surf pulsed,
wrapping time around us.

How long ago was that – when we
were sanctuary for each other –
drying tidal pools, rescuing sand
castles our only concerns?

Beaches drown with memories
of how we chased the spume,
danced on caramel sand.
I've buried a sister, a friend.
When was the family string cut –
who brought the knife?

Far from Madrid

Albescent waves finger the shore,
jostle sand so sunsets shimmer,
shift in a Moroccan dance.

Shearwaters, petrels peel lovers
away from the city where fragments
of acacias shelter cobbled streets.

Only a bed and a blanket of blue here.

STURGEON MOON
August

Twilight casts its net, and palmettos
spider the Carolina sky. Swirling
reds, oranges descend like an anchor,
reel in shadows, hinge the black tide.

Mayflies bait the brackish night
and beckon the mounting moon. Sand
spins and knots as water quicksilvers
the shoals. In the flats, spot tails
and tarpon angle through eddies, waves
unspool against the coast.

                Inland,
new corn fins earthen canals, air
moist with summer. Peridot husks
silk golden kernels that glisten like roe.
A farmer trolls soil channels, son
watching from a docked tractor as grain
grins obscenely. Stars blister the sky.

ELEMENTAL

Forget the myths of El Dorado: youth and health,
unspoiled land guarded by magic and holy men.
Wealth, pleasure waiting for any who braved the sea
king with wood and cloth. A land worth gold.

Six hundred years and the city lurks in inky black
on the eastern shore, but lights line the boulevard;
jai lai arenas, strip clubs highlighted in neon.

Sirens shriek over vagabonds, predators spoiling
these Miami streets – sleeping, dealing under the palms.
Oleanders sag in the heat tourists seek.

                    Today's sun glimmered over the deep.
Underwater currents ripped and rolled, spumed salty spray
as waves thudded the shore, plastered sidewalks. Salt sharpened
the air, stabbed nostrils, filmed bodies pacing the boulevards.

                                             But tonight

Poseidon sleeps, trident quieting the tide. The sea is chaste,
wavelets teasing the sand. Clouds disrobe a splinter of moon.

Dante Meets Katrina, 2005

"Death could scarce be bitterer." Inferno, *Canto I*

Condensation beads the rim
of the dome, both top and bottom,
even the walls start to sweat –
mercury beginning to rise
here in the anteroom to hell.
Wind howls, solid steel separates,
tears like tissue: a metamorphosis
has occurred; no Virgil to guide
our exploration of this underworld
on earth. We tremble on the fringe,
unveiled wails rising from those souls
who sought refuge, thought the inner
circle would be safe.

And it's still raining . . .

We pass plastic seats sticky
with yesterday's soda,
today's tissues; the stench
of diapers unchanged, body odor
saturates every particle of air;
men play checkers, insensible
to the chaos; a clothesline strung
across rows airs a musty, molding
blanket. Deeper we descend
where teenagers carve graffiti,
where artists scrawl torn trees,
open roofs, floating dogs.

And it's still raining . . .

The center of this storm silent.
And cold. One woman rocks
herself while red seeps
from her puffy lip, torn dress
covers bruised knees; a child stares
ahead, mouth moving, voiceless;
an old man sits yoga-style beating
his head into the moist, thick air.
Others converge, a brawl
beginning to brew in the tangle
of bodies.

It's still raining . . .

HURRICANE
– for Michelle

Sea growls against the rotting dock,
blistered boards collapse into white lather
as Andrew flies into sand, mortar, bone.

Hasty clouds blink back sun. Winds reel,
a plaintiff to somnolent autumn days.

Storm whines, shrieks – the house
shudders, foundation shifting. Dishes stutter,
pictures and knickknacks tremble.

Then everything holds its breath.

St Augustine, Early Morning

Dark, hushed
light seeps over the pulsing horizon
as the sun sneaks into the sky,
hides behind filmy clouds that tremble
into vapor. Waves rake the sandbar
then glide onto the still beach.
Shells fleck the shoreline as whiting play
leap frog in the shallows.

Dim shapes
break the wide, yawning blue –
a pelican lumbers north, and three terns follow
its wake, skim white crests as they dance
across the sky. A dark fin, then another breaks
the surface – dolphins tunnel through the surf,
feed in the dawn.

A fishing boat chugs in. Offshore, a cabin cruiser
shuts off its running lights, slides into the haze.

FROM TWO TO ONE

Summers were best, daylight yawned early,
stayed awake late. When sun skimmed
the rooftops, we jumped rope, hopscotch
out front – girl games, I know, but he didn't
seem to mind. A swing set near the chain
link fence tented Jacob and me, sand shifting

between our toes, Miami air a sticky breath.
We turned flips over metal bars, blistered
our legs on its blue and white paint,
tried to out-swing each other. Across the street,
shades drawn after ten, house kept chill
and dim, kitchen linoleum anchored

the Sit-n-Spin for twirling contests, his yarmulke
whirling. Ivory cushions and carpet blurred,
latkes, salami swirled our nostrils. Saturdays
were doll days. No other children on our street,
Jacob's family at synagogue – his mother clucking
him into the car. But those lingering weekdays

were ours, cooling in the canal bordering my backyard.
Years after my family moved north, I heard an alligator
crawled from that canal nudging her eggs by the saw-
grass that separated interstate and suburb. She was exiled
to the Everglades . . . . When we left, Jacob,
I didn't cry for the house or the yard or the swing.

Daybreak at the Old City Park

Eight mallards bathe in the stagnant lake,
nodding, tossing spray over downy backs,
a carnival atmosphere in the dry, still air.
They ignore my trek past their early shower.

Farther along in the wood I linger by a circle
of concrete, filled in and feral with ivy.
A forgotten fountain? Out by the highway
cars hum and a train clatters its tracks.

Caramel-colored pine needles dust the moss,
and I head toward the fading water. Wrinkled
cans, old bottles, even a pair of muddy galoshes
unveil to the deer nosing their way to the bank.

No clouds again today. No hope of rain.
Gnats swarm the scum that stipples olive
water, and pines lean for a drink. Canada geese
yak, one hisses me from her golden-necked

goslings. Reeds rattle as the birds feed, try to nest.
A cloud of swallows ink the gathering blue,
and a woodpecker knocks on an oak overhead.
King of the lake, a heron poses on a log.

He gapes, admires his likeness, then darts
his beak, fracturing the surface.

PURGATORY

Sibilance silenced, parched
riverbed masquerades
as ditch – margins crazed
and cracked, gilded
with knots of leaves, grass.

Noon sun sears seething
blue August.

Splintered, a cask shores
the river's bank like a boat,
Stygian route impassable,
impossible. We are marooned
in antiphonal quiet.

The bank bears its burden.
We wait for the river to fill.

SUMMER IN CLIMAX

Bees lumber over clover by the river
in the south Georgia heat. No air blows
through the sultry shade as twilight ruins
the all-blue sky, cloudless since noon.
We simmer on the porch, breathless, severe
with words, savoring any puff of breath.

Granny snaps a *Moonshine Kills* hand fan, breathing
currents of quick, warm wind. And the river
trembles under dotted sun and shadow, Sevier
Basin drying, waiting for a squall to blow.
Sapped from their swim in the lake at noon,
the kids sprawl on cotton sheets, ruined

by years of towel duty and plucking rue in
season. Tongues flapped out, the dogs try to breathe,
heads and tails drooped like flowers at noon.
Fireflies swap places with bees by the river,
where a few lively boys try to grab them, blowing
their wings to light the deepening night less severely

than bare bulbs. Porch lights off, no moth wings sever
this summer night. Flies gather around the ruins
of soda and lemonade. In the sluggish air, Sissy blows
damp hair from my face, teasing tendrils with her breath.
Crickets and frogs compete by the river's
edge – a stereo of sound that will be silent by noon.

Even with drinks and fans, the porch is as warm as noon.
The moon, brilliant and globed, creates sharp shadows, severely
outlining the house. The melody of rocks and river
splashes into night music. No one wants to ruin
the spell with speech, but we step inside to breathe
without mosquitoes, sweating, waiting for the wind to blow.

I dream of shaded skies, storms blowing
the heat east – somewhere far away by noon.
We'll visit on the porch, take damp breaths
of clover and watch the rain tumble in, thrusting severe
currents down drain spouts; we'll laugh at the ruined
wash on the line as clouds renew the river.

Rain runches the river. Abandoned leaves blow,
ruined green jewels shimmering in the pale noon.
A severe gust scoots them downstream, brings us breath.

Autumnal Equinox

Harvest Moon
September

Ragged stalks burr the dirt,
scraps fallen from tractors,
abandoned by hands that came
behind. Moonlight voids night,
floods the dusking field, hours
before bursting, ripe.

Spider spirals gather dew, thread
through asters and bedded morning
glories, wink at the moon, rival
the stars. Barns gorge with hay,
pumpkins spill onto dance floors.
An owl swivels its ruff,

last gasp of summer.

Morning Dew

Cocooned in mist breathing
beads of dew, the day begins.
Hope lightens my heart like vapor
that rises on an autumn morning.
Cool tendrils of fog envelope my face,
my body. I see myself absorbed
into the blinding whiteness of this day.

Silence.

No sound touches me here –
my own private paradise.
Fuzzy outlines loom closer,
darker as I walk on: just trees,
sentinels of the wood shimmering
with wet pearls of dew. The path
blurs and focuses. From beyond
the shifting wall of white, robins
chirp and squirrels rustle
the underbrush, crackling leaves
like explosions in the eerie quiet,
reminder of the day ahead.

LAUNCHING SEPTEMBER

Wind has worn the trees
to gnarled gnomes, foot
soldiers in these woods.
Along the edges, drooping
plums halo morning glories,
echo a paler shade of sky.

Pines sweat summer's
end, casualties with seeping
wounds. One anvil-like stump
hosts mycelia, mushrooms
blossom in knotty creases.
Ants besiege fading blooms –
mad creatures crawling
through past lives.

September Woods

Mount Kearsarge curves over Warner,
and those last summer days silver
my memory. You and the boys
training Max to catch, Frisbee
coated with doggy-slobber, watermelon
oozing juice on the picnic table.

Then vacant pillows of thought
descend, a merciful amnesia
to the tantrum of car horns, rubber
and metal shrieking against asphalt.

A break between skull, vertebrae
and you're gone.

Up at Rollins Park, hemlocks hedge
the oak, butternut. Wedged beneath a fading
roof, fronds spiral, green faceted ferns
brightening bark. Leaves gasp, chatter in wind.
Days cool, condense.
Soon the branches will be bare,
all that's left evergreen.

Hunter's Moon
October

Piercing the deep blue
of midnight, a scarecrow
– crucified – rises above
the razored field, blanches
under the moon's full light.
Fox tracks dent stiffening
dirt, vanish with whispering
leaves. In the quiet a buck
grunts, opals scale the sky.

Modern Alchemy

Shards of sunlight pierce leaves
this late afternoon. Light effervesces,
grapples with shadow. Golden oak,
maples russet and ginger spill
in all directions, path erased.
I'm lost.

The feral trail funneled into an orchard
grown wild. Tufts of grass crowd knotted
apple, straight-limbed lime, spiral with spider
webs. But the quince tree, tenacious,
bursts upward, green fruit yellows, flames
the darkling sky.

Fog spools low, white sheets smoothing
the rough-hewn turf. Day fades
as leaves flinch with whippoorwills.
I hunker down to wait the dawn. Crickets
pluck the air, and a mockingbird piccolos
notes to twilight's sonata.

Crisping wind harvests mossy clues
and owl hoots, moon not yet risen
above the foothills.

Redirection of Light

Summer's green suit morphs
into jeweled robes – topaz and ruby
winking from tree tops, bleached corn
fields razed to stubble, withered apples
worming the ground.

                  Crows stab both
bittersweet and writhing flesh, strut
through an atlas of leaves – boundaries
blurring, altering with the wind.

October's sun too fleeting to fortify
the earth, mother moon full and rising.

FLUX

Sun rises from the river,
pale echo of evening's bold release.
Wavelets runch the surface
as I slow the car over the bridge.

A blue heron unfolds from her perch
on a channel marker, her pearls
shining in the crooked, reeded nest.
She tackles the water, rises with trout.

A fisherman casts his line, body
a silhouette on the glittering river.
Water rushes the shore, kisses
the bank where black-eyed susans bend.

I wanted you to call yesterday, fell asleep
with the phone. The ache in my neck
twinges as sun smolders the sky.

. . . IN A BOTTLE

A tangerine sunrise bruises the sky,
annihilating night on an altar of ocean.

Mid-autumn, the beach is empty.
Wind tangles sea oats, frosts waves
as they smack the shore.

                    Farther out,
in hazy light, two fins break the bumpy
surface. Water sprays the lightening
sky.

Translation

Ridges wrinkle, hem these Tennessee
valleys, explode with russet, gold.
Maples shake titian heads into orange,
burning into blue.

Autumn bursts into the mountains,
bold, unlike Spring who blushes
one blossom at a time. Air chills,
swollen and earthy with walnut, oak.

Growing up under a flat Florida sun
whose fall births only hurricanes,
I witnessed blue horizons –
sea and sky a yawning mirror.

No gulls or sea oats penetrate the pines
shivering here in October air. Sun crawls
the foothills, silhouettes the valley in ashen
shadows, colors brushed under dusk.

BREACHING THE DEPTHS
– Fajardo, Puerto Rico

Sunlight gathers, shifts
in lightning shafts across
and through the blue.

Camera can't capture purpling
Blue Tangs, lobsters embedded
in sand, hazy rays glutted with plankton.

Stroking liquid air, I touch my toes
in an underwater dive. Bubbles tickle
my face, hide angle fish flashing past.

Gorgonian coral and sea fans sway
in the swell, undulate around rock-still
brain coral oblivious to the tide.

Boat floating above, no sound
breaches the depths – just my body
shrouded with pulsing pressure.

Blue stretches into black, waiting.

MOVING

Balsam blue sifts daylight
through open frames – doors
and windows once more bare –
an empty box waiting to be filled
with treasures again. No longer
home, I close yesterday's door.
The lock clicks.

The vacant pier slouches under
butternut, pine, oak. Leaves drop
like copper coins from a rich man's hand,
breeze sputtering them onto the pond.
Offerings of color tap its quiet surface.
Frogs nuzzle into mud, mums fold
winter within their petals.

Beaver Moon

November

A colony of stars splinters the sky,
lodges with a low yellow moon
as it swims in frosty air. The archer
tightens his bow, tramples scorpion
whose stinger burrows into horizon.
Ice furs the fields and doves mutter,
trapped in sleep.

       Poplars, bark gnawed
to the belly, sutured with kudzu and ice,
sprawl by the shallows. Chrysanthemum
petals settle like silken snow flakes,
confuse feathering lake with night sky –
universe mirrored in black and white.

Thanksgiving

Fog mantles the fading moon
as morning gray dissolves the dark.

Fir trees bristle the sky with vague
silhouettes. My back to the scaling sun,

I drive away from you, heart folding,
collapsing into a sorrow I can't shake.

Late November branches scratch the gathering
blue. A few brown leaves sag in the wind.

I slow the car. Family waits at the end
of this journey. Turkey, candles, wine

centerpiece the table. A whole day planned
together – babies and dogs and . . .

I pull off the road – edge splintered
with pieces of rubber, stones –

take a breath, turn toward home.

Incandescent

Clouds nibble the moon,
rays fading as rain wrinkles the sky.

I fumble with matches, desire
more than darkness of soul. I look

for you in the unlit shadows. Candles
prick the room, yellow glow conceding hope.

I wait.

FROST LINE

It doesn't take much, does it,
for the mountain to meet the moon,
flawless globe snagging the jagged
rock. Rising only inches higher
through the night, the frosty moon
blinks as dark clouds polish
its surface and dust stars
close in the November sky.

COLD MOON

December

Sea-goat and archer tussle
above silent pines, holly
clusters huddling under quilts
of snow. High and white,
light gluts the cliffs, merges
them with ocean, black and slick
as oil. Stars asterisk the sky, faint
memories of July's moon vine.

Wind pricks numbed fields,
shivers the window frames
on this long night. Shadows stretch
hoary fingers through the glass.
The swollen globe pauses
behind a cloud. Listen for its light.

REFRAIN

Twilight calls. Crickets hum,
frogs chirrup and light pinpricks
the sky. Moon hangs low
still unseen behind the pines, dark
silhouettes against the horizon.

Love was a night like this:
kisses teased away the day,
supper cooked over campfire
then your guitar, your voice
cradling me to sleep.

Nights like tonight, I listen
for your song in the whispering
trees. Wait for the moon to rise.

Pocket Wilderness

We wander these woods
for the perfect spot. Bare
branches lace overhead,
a few tremulous leaves
crackling close to bark.

Late morning rays fortify
the December air but can't
quite catch shadows
nestled into crevices near
the coal mine. Black,
iridescent crumbs beckon
the curious, the unwary,
inside its rotting corpse.

Red tic-tac-toes graffiti
sandstone by the waterfall,
the carapace from millennia
when these woods sheltered
beneath the sea.

Ahead, sunshine polarizes,
blurs reality, and time whispers
through creaking elm and oak.
We pause by the pulsing
falls, faces freezing
under flying fragments of light.

About the Author

KB Ballentine teaches English and theatre arts to high school and college students when she's not writing. She has attended writing academies in both America and Britain. Published in *Bent Pin, MO: Writings from the River, Sequoia Review, River Poets Journal* and *Naugatuck River Review*, she shares her work in various poetry groups. In 2006 she was a finalist for the Joy Harjo Poetry Award and in 2006 and 2007 was awarded prizes from the Dorothy Sargent Rosenberg Memorial Fund. KB has a B.A. and M.A. in Writing and a MFA in Creative Writing and Poetry. Readers can contact KB via her website: www.kbballentine.com.

About the Book

The titles and subtitles are set in Copperplate, with the text of the poems in Georgia. The paper is 55 lbs with a 10 pt laminated cover. Interior design and cover by Greyhound Books. The cover photograph, taken by the author, features three peaks known as "The Three Sisters." They are located in the Dingle Peninsula, County Kerry, Ireland. The photograph of the author was taken by Janie Sheldon.

CELTIC CAT PUBLISHING

Celtic Cat Publishing was founded in 1995 to publish emerging and established writers.

The following works are available from Celtic Cat Publishing at www.celticcatpublishing.com, from Amazon.com and from major bookstores.

Poetry

Exile: Poems of an Irish Immigrant, James B. Johnston

Marginal Notes, Frank Jamison

Rough Ascension and Other Poems of Science, Arthur J. Stewart

Bushido: The Virtues of Rei and Makoto, Arthur J. Stewart

Ebbing & Flowing Springs: New and Selected Poems and Prose (1976-2001), Jeff Daniel Marion

Gathering Stones, KB Ballentine

Humor

My Barbie Was an Amputee, Angie Vicars

Life Among the Lilliputians, Judy Lockhart DiGregorio

Chanukah

One for Each Night: Chanukah Tales and Recipes, Marilyn Kallet

Printed in the United States
220282BV00005B/1/P